D0246992

moshi1024555

billandcag

mouse127921

diamondintellect

SUNBIRD

Published by Ladybird Books Ltd 2012
A Penguin Company
Penguin Books Ltd, 80 Strand, London, WC2R 0RL, UK
Penguin Group (USA) Inc., 375 Hudson Street, New York 10014, USA
Penguin Books Australia Ltd, Camberwell Road, Camberwell, Victoria 3124,
Australia (A division of Pearson Australia Group Pty Ltd)
Penguin Group (NZ), 67 Apollo Drive, Rosedale, Auckland 0632,
New Zealand (a division of Pearson New Zealand Ltd)
Canada, India, South Africa

Sunbird is a trade mark of Ladybird Books Ltd

Written by Mandy Archer and Steve Cleverley. Illustrations by Vincent Bechet,
Ross McCaughey, Lea Wade and Trevor White.

Comic by Kieran Grant with illustrations by Fran Brylewska

www.ladybird.com

ISBN: 978-1-40939-1029
001 - 10 9 8 7 6 5 4 3 2 1
Printed in China

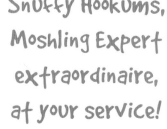

Snuffy Hookums,
Moshling Expert
extraordinaire,
at your service!

Contents

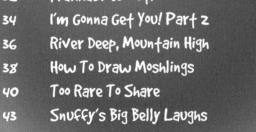

Snuffy's Journal

Day 1,879

Drifted for yet more aimless miles. Looked up at the stars wondering what my mentor Buster Bumblechops would do in a sitch like this. Haven't seen the old boy since we landed in that spot of bother at Mount Krakkablowa 1,879 days ago.

Day 1,874

Breakfast: A mug of Slop and a slug of Bug Juice.

Morning: Got chased into the water by a vine-swinging troop of Cheeky Chimps.

Lunch: None

Afternoon: Found everything I needed to whittle a raft out of floating driftwood. Had to act fast, the chimps were pelting me with banana skins. I calculated that it would only be a matter of minutes before they moved onto coconut shells.

Supper: Fried Oobla Doobla

Evening: After a daring escape, my raft drifted out onto open sea. I soon found myself floating alone on Potion Ocean.

Days 1,875-7
Drifting, drifting, drifting . . .

Day 1,880

Land ahoy at last! Rubbed my eyes. Could that really be the bustling boardwalk of The Port glinting in the distance? It is?! Cool beanz! Brace yourself Monstro City, Snuffy Hookums is coming home!!

Day 1,881

A tantalising wait as the gentle waves of Potion Ocean lightly lap me towards The Port. The last time I was in town, I was assistant to top Moshling collector Buster Bumblechops. If I hadn't got lost on that fateful Krakkablowa expedition I'd still be his trusty sidekick today! Not that I regret it - I discovered a stack of stuff during my time in the wilds. Now I need to get back to Buster and share my research.

Day 1,878

Bumped my raft into a most obliging Batty Bubblefish. Took things carefully - everyone knows that an angry Bubblefish will splurt galloons of gloop if it gets angry. Offered to trade one of my old flip-flops in return for directions to the nearest landmass. Blurp agreed, but then couldn't remember its way home. Shucks!

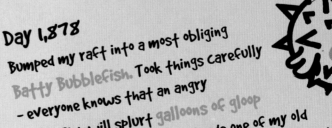

A=
B=
C=
D=
E=
F=
G=
H=
I=
J=
K=
L=
M=
N=
O=
P=
Q=
R=
S=
T=
U=
V=
W=
X=
Y=
Z=

Can you help me get to the ranch? Every time you find a pictogram, decode it and write the letter on page 55.

To my dear Snuffy (the best sidekick any Moshlingologist could wish for, sniff!),

Keep this paper safe, it holds the key to my ranch. Well not actually the key to the ranch, but the key to finding the key to my ranch (ahem). I've hidden twenty-four pictograms across Monstro City. You'll need to track down all of them to reveal my location.

My Moshlings and I will be waiting and hoping.

Travel safely!

Day 1,882

The Port looms ever closer. Lucky thing too, I'm down to my last Garlic Marshmallow. Once I get back on dry land, I must puzzle out the location of Buster's ranch. It's such a closely guarded secret, even Buster gets lost on his way home some days! Gotta stay like that too – Dr. Strangeglove and his evil Glump minions would wreak Moshling havoc if they cracked his cover.

Some say locating the ranch is as tricky as finding a Hoodoo in a haystack. I'd have to agree, if it wasn't for the screwed-up ball of paper Buster slipped into my rucksack during our last moments together.

MY MARVELLOUS MONSTAR

All the time spent alone in the wilds has made me forget my manners I haven't even asked about YOU yet! Do excuse me. Fill in the form using your most monstrous handwriting, and I'll add your deets to my research. Don't leave anything out, Moshling collectors are always fascinated by new case studies.

My Moshi And Me

Owner's name:

My Monster's name:

Draw a picture of your monster here.

Personality:

My monster likes:

My monster dislikes:

Favourite Moshling:

M◯nsters In Sight!

Fascinating stuff, your Monster is a fine specimen! It's great to meet a like-minded Moshi maniac. Fancy joining me on my hike across Monstro City? I could do with some help searching for Buster's ranch and when I last checked, the post of Snuffy's sidekick was currently vacant!

Interested? Before we get started, let's put your monster know-how to the test. Can you identify each of these Moshis? Study the view through my spinoculars, then write the correct name beneath each one.

1.

2.

3.

4.

5.

6.

9

Fishies Tank

YOU WILL NEED

A brown cardboard box
Sticky tape
Pencil
Ruler
Safety scissors
White cardboard
Paint brush
Poster paint
Sheet of paper
Cotton or fishing wire
PVA glue
Sand

During those days drifting aimlessly across Potion ocean, I never stopped studying the Fishies that splashed past my raft. Want to help me make a tank to display these squelchtastic Moshlings? A few simple steps will show you how to make the best fishie tank ever without even getting soggy!

WHAT TO DO

1.

Tape the box closed and then lie it flat on the table. Use a pencil and ruler to draw a rectangular window on each side of the box. Make sure that you don't place the frames too close to the edge.

2.

Carefully cut out the frames so that your box has a large window on all four sides. Put your tank to one side.

3.

Using the Fishies on this page for inspiration, draw some Fishies for your tank on a piece of white card, then carefully cut them out. Make two for each Moshling so that you can stick the two sides together later.

4.

Find a brush, then paint your Fishies in bright colours. While they are drying, paint your tank inside and out. You could even decorate it with Moshi stickers!

5.

When your tank is dry, lay a sheet of paper over the base of the box. Carefully push a pencil through the paper, creating a hole for each of the Fishies you have made. Now turn the box over and lay the same piece of paper over the top. Pierce through the same points again so that you have matching holes at the top and bottom.

6.

Thread a length of pale cotton or fishing wire through the first hole at the base of the tank and tie a knot underneath. Run the thread up and out through the top, securing it with another tight knot. Repeat for each set of holes.

7.

Take two matching Moshling shapes and lay them on your work surface coloured-side down. Dot PVA glue around the edges, then push the shapes together around the tank's first vertical line of thread. Do the same with the rest of the Fishies, setting the critters at differing heights in the 'water'.

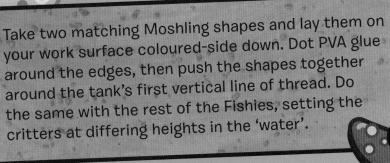

8.

When your tank is full of splashing Seastars and Batty Bubblefish, you're ready to put it on display. Sprinkle a layer of sand at the bottom, stand back and enjoy!

Cap'n Buck's Port Tour

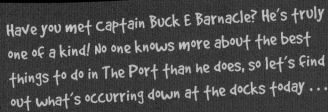

Have you met Captain Buck E Barnacle? He's truly one of a kind! No one knows more about the best things to do in The Port than he does, so let's find out what's occurring down at the docks today . . .

Y'aaarrgggghhh!

Hello, me hearties. Any friend of Snuffy is a friend of mine! Follow me and I'll show youse landlubbers all sorts of salty secrets.

BABS' BOUTIQUE

Aye, aye! No visit to The Port would be complete without dropping into good 'ol Babs'. Her hair be one of the wonders of the Moshi world – swears by using floor wax to get her look, she does! Babs' shop is choccy-bloccy-woccy full of rare items to buy.

Cloudy Cloth Clipper

My old mate Roary Scrawl will let ye know when I'm docking the *Cloudy Cloth Clipper* down at The Port. Ye can guarantee I'll have some great booty on board from my travels across the Seventy Seas!

SUPER SEEDS

Y'arrggh, do you be a Moshling fan my new friend? Ye are? Well, ye best head to our finest Moshling seed shop then! Shiver me timbers if you can't get all ye need here to grow a mega-list of Moshlings!

12

Colorama

Is yer monster's coat looking sleepier than a Disco Duckie after a non-stop sesh on the dance floor? Best get over to Colorama for a spruce up!

PAWS'N'CLAWS

Gilbert Finnster is proper Moshling mental! Ever since he were mini he's dedicated his life to selling the finest Moshling codes and memorabilia. Don't go in if you're in a hurry, mind. He's a natterbox is Finnster. He's got more jibber than a school full of jabberers!

Cap'n Buck's Guide To Giving Dr. Strangeglove The Slip

If I were in charge, I'd make naughty 'ol Glove-y guts take a swim with the sharks, but don't tell him I said that! Until I do get to turn the tables, I stay out of Dr. Strangeglove's way. Here are some quick tricks for making yerself invisibobble, too!

Disguises

If Dr. Strangeglove can't see ye, he can't find ye! Pop to the Colorama for a change of look, or head over to Tyra Fangs' spa salon for a makeover. Disguises work a treat too! Head over to the Dress Up Shop near Main Street – an eye patch and a pirate's hat is a smashing place to start!

Secret Codes

Dr. Strangeglove's evil all right, but he's no dope. Finding a way to read yer notes and letters is well within his means. Make sure he won't understand what you've scrawled by agreeing a code with your hearties. Ye can use mine if you like until ye get yer own. I switch each letter of the alphabet to a number. A becomes 1, B becomes 2, C equals 3 and so on.

Use the code to work out this message.

13 25 14 1 13 5 9 19 3 1 16'14 2 21 3 11

GOING UNDERGROUND

Stories of my moshpeditions seem to have made me something of a minor celeb back home. To celebrate my return, I've been invited, along with a host of V.I.M.s (Very Important Moshis) for a party at the exclusive Underground Disco!

I do have one problem though – I've seen newborn Performing flappasaurus with better rhythm than I have! Please help. My friend Max Volume has given me some boogie tips and a dance routine to get me started. Let's learn it together!

Max Volume's Groove Tips

Dancing is a cinch! Any Moshi can do it. Just use my tricks of the boogie trade . . .

You don't need a dance floor to get down, but you do need some space. Enough room to swing Gingersnap the Whinger Cat should do it.

Make sure you're loose and relaxed - you'll end up looking like Mini Ben the Teeny TickTock if you try to dance with a stiff body. Shake your arms and legs out until you feel relaxed and ready.

Okay, now the important bit. No matter what the Moshi Music is, it'll have a regular beat you can tap your foot along to. Bend your legs along with that beat, stomp your feet to it, clap your hands, sway your hips, try any movement you feel like trying. As long as you keep to the beat, it'll look great.

Be confident and enjoy it. Doesn't it feel good?

MOSHI MANIA ROUTINE

Find your favourite Moshi Music tune and crank it up LOUD! This routine should work with any music. Bubba's got 'Moptop Tweenybop' by Zack Binspin on his eyePod right now.

Step three

Keep clapping and clicking to the beat, but now put one foot in front of the other so that you're swaying forwards and backwards.

Step one

Stand with your feet apart, moving your weight from one foot to the other, in time to the music.

Step two

Keep swaying from side to side in time to the song but now add a clap above your head, followed by a click of your fingers on every other beat.

Step Four

The last step! Keep moving forwards and backwards and clapping in time, but instead of a finger click to the beat, make an M shape with your arms. If you're feeling extra confident you can lay down some freestyle moves or shout "Moshi" with every step!

High five! You've just learnt the Moshi Mania dance!

10   10   10

15

Frenzy in Flutterby Field

Goodness me, there's Colonel Catcher! I'm a big fan of his. We share a lot in common – both being intrepid, resourceful explorers (even if I do say so myself!) on the hunt for new species. Where my specialty is Moshlings, Colonel Catcher is a flutterby expert. He's the best in his field!

How many Flutterbies can you catch in Flutterby Field? One of them is rarer than all the others, which is it?

Snuffy, my dear girl! How good to see you! May I compliment you on your impeccable timing – the lid has fallen off of my specimen jar and my Flutterbies have flapped off. Can you help me find them? Some of them are very rare, my dear, there's no time to waste!

Meander Down MAIN STREET ⬇

Now the flutterbies are safely back in their jar, the Colonel has offered to give us a guided tour of Main Street. It's changed so much since I last mooched down Main!

COLONEL CATCHER'S MAIN STREET DOS AND DO, DO, DOS!

Do
Find greedy grots Bjorn Squish, he's always nabbing a quiet spot to grab a quick Moshi munch!

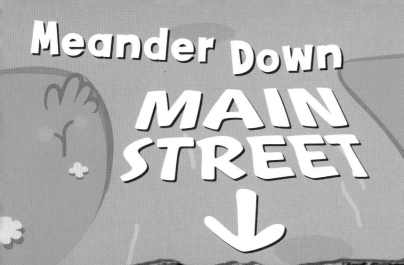

Do
Make some time to go Moshling Boshling – it's catchier than a case of the Moshi measles! Just look out for the Picnicking pair Pete and Lila, they'll show you where to go.

Do, Do, Do
Make friends! There's always someone to chat to on Main Street. I myself have met some fascinating monsters there over the years.

ROSS-ERY STORE

MOSHLING SEEDS

FLUTTERBY FIELD

OPEN

Do, Do, Do
Visit all the shops. They are fine establishments indeed! Just follow me . . .

17

YUKEA

Yukea stocks everything you need for a home makeover. Pop in and grab the wallpaper, lights and furniture to turn your place into the funkiest freakhome ever!

GROSS-ERY STORE

If you're hankering for some Chocolate-covered Broccoli, desperate to dine on a slice of Roarberry Cheesecake or simply thirsty for a glass of bootiful Bug Juice then this is the joint for you! Storeowner Snozzle Wobbleson has every monster munch-up you could ever dream of.

EN GEN

No entry here without a hard hat! Inside, Chief EN-GENeer Dizzee Bolt is keeping Monstro City supplied with power.

BIZARRE BAZAAR

Hmmm, how to describe the BB's wares? Let's just say 'unusual'. Whether it's an Eye TV set, a tribal Uno mask or a simple Hornament, every item on sale does share one thing in common – it's uggerly fangtastic!

The Daily Growl

What a fine publication, my dear. I really don't know how I would keep up with all the daily ooze without it! I understand the editor, Roary Scrawl, has reported on your incredible Moshcoveries, Snuffy. Let's pop in and take a look at the latest issue...

Roar All About It!

Wing, Fang, Screech and Sonar, I've only gone and made the FRONT PAGE! I guess that makes me a celebrity, not that I'm bothered, of course. But hold on one mo, Roary Scrawl's printer doesn't seem to be working properly. Some of the words and pictures are missing. Can you fill them in for me so that everyone knows my story? Like I say, not that bothered, of course!

The Daily Growl

All the ooze that's fit to print!

Intrepid Moshling hunter Snuffy Hookums dramatically returned to Monstro City today after _____ days on her own in the wild! Her reappearance has put paid to rumours that she had been eaten by a tribe of dangerous Moshlings somewhere near Mount _____ .

Hookums' incredible return will be celebrated with a monstermental boogie party at the _____ _____ . Crowds have been warned to get there early to avoid being left out in the cold.

The Moshling expert is yet to speak publicly of her incredible experience. But, when she does, *The Daily Growl* will as usual be the furriest with the story!

Continued . . .

_____
_____
_____

Snuffy Hookums, pictured with mentor Buster Bumblechops, shortly before her disappearance.

19

Pete and Lila's Potty Picnic

You could blow me down with a flap of a Flutterby's wings – it's Snuffy! I'd hoped I would see you. How are you? I've added some slime-tastic slugs to my collection while you've been away. I can't get enough of the slippery suckers!

Speaking of suckers, Snuffs, have you run into any Glumps since you've been back in town? The little villains are causing B-I-G problems.

It would be a good idea to learn the Glumps' names, so you can stay well clear. I've got a little quiz that should help. Why don't you sit down, suck on a Spider Lolly and give it a go?

How thrilling to be front-page news! I think I'll take the Colonel's advice and catch up with Pete and Lila for a quick chat.

GLUMP HUNT!

Eight Glump names are mumbled and jumbled up in the word grid, can you find them? The names could be running in any direction, even back to front!

M	U	S	T	A	C	H	I	O	B
Y	J	B	X	I	L	O	E	B	P
G	G	B	C	L	J	S	V	R	L
F	I	S	H	L	I	P	S	U	K
A	E	B	L	M	Y	O	J	I	B
B	G	H	B	O	R	D	T	S	L
I	F	Y	K	U	V	G	F	E	O
O	E	C	R	B	N	E	D	R	O
W	O	S	L	U	P	T	C	L	P
R	P	A	S	Q	U	I	N	F	Y

FISHLIPS
BLOOPY
ROCKO
PODGE
FABIO
MUSTACHIO
BRUISER
NED

All present and correct! Now see if you can name another four of Strangeglove's minions.

1. _____
2. _____
3. _____
4. _____

Stroll Along
OOH LA LANE

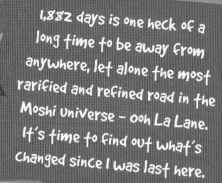

1,882 days is one heck of a long time to be away from anywhere, let alone the most rarified and refined road in the Moshi universe – Ooh La Lane. It's time to find out what's changed since I was last here.

Tyra's Spa

Tyra Fangs has one aim in life – to make the Moshi population as beautiful as she is! She gives miraculous makeovers in her exclusive spa. Perhaps you could pop in and help give her clients a Slop facepack?

ICE-SCREAM!

Monsters love Ice-Scream, so there's always jobs going at Giuseppe Gelato's store. If you are a dab hand at dishing out desserts there could be some Rox in it for you!

GOOGENHEIM ART GALLERY

Drop into the Gallery to submit your Moshiest pictures and get inspiration for new designs.

PRINT WORKSHOP

Learn how to draw your own perfect Moshi Monster, make a mask, print a poster, try out some trading cards and oodles more.

NEW HOUSES

This superstore is packed to the rafters with houses in every style. Fancy kipping in a Skyscraper or living happily ever after in a Fairytale Castle? You got it!

Hidden Delights

Ooh La Lane is filled with hidden extras. See if you can work out how to make the street lamps swing, or stop by and make a monster wish at the well. Can you find the hidden entrance to the Underground Disco, the most exclusive nightclub in the whole city?

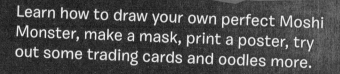

TYRA FANGS' MONSTER MAKEOVER

Roaming the jungle was great for my study of Moshlings, but not so hot for my hair! Join me for a full blown pampering session at Tyra Fangs' Spa. She's famous for her miracle monster makeovers.

> Darlings!
> Welcome to my spa.
> Ooh, you are in a state! Never fear, I'll have you looking fierce and furry in no time. Let me show you the tools of my trade . . .

TYRA'S TOOLS

TWEEZERS – There are no short cuts if you want to look fabulous like me! Getting that roarway-ready look takes time. Every treatment at my salon starts with the tweezers, it really is the only way to get muck out of the fur.

GOOP FOR MONSTERS – Once I've picked all the mud off (oh the glamour!), it's time for a thorough scrubbing with a good quality soap. We only use the best at Tyra Fangs' Spa, and it doesn't come any better than Goop for Monsters. It's made from only the finest ingredients and then hung from vines in Sniggerton Wood for exactly 362 days before it's ready to use. It has to be exactly 362 days though. I used one that had hung a day too long once - it permed every hair on my face!

SLOP FACEPACK – Next up is a mudpack facial. Ours use Croak Creek bank mud, it smells awful but there's none better!

RELAX – While your facepack dries we always chillax our clients. Put your feet up and bury your head in a copy of *MonSTAR Monthly* magazine or enjoy the sniffs and snuffs of a whiffy candle. Scent of rotting rubbish is my total favourite!

BLOW-DRY – Nearly done! After rinsing off your face pack, we'll bouff your do with a quick blow-dry.

STINK! EAU DE SOCKS – A quick spritz of Stink! and you're done! You look like a new monster . . . and smell like an old one!

Draw Snuffy after her makeover!
Barbecued Bubblefish, what a
monSTAR!

IT'S A MODERN MONSTER WORLD

I was just a young Moshlingologist the last time I was in Monstro City, but I did have connections! My royal friends Prince Sillyham and Kate Giggleton (who I knew before she became a princess) were top of my speed dial. Now the royal pair have promised to introduce me to the new monster it crowd!

Prince Sillyham And Kate Giggleton — Fast Factz

◆ Prince Sillyham is genuine Moshi royalty. He lists his hobbies as adjusting his crown, riding his magical mule and driving around in a Rox-encrusted royal carriage.

◆ Kate Giggleton can often be spotted lunching with her gal pals on Ooh La Lane.

◆ Prince Sillyham has a team of monsters whose job it is to ensure his pillows are always plumped 'just so'.

◆ Kate has become mega-rich since marrying into royalty. But, despite all the Rox to her name, she never carries money!

Snuffy sweetie, good to see you! Have a glass of bubbleade and meet some of my chums. Tally-ho!

THE 'IT' CROWD

Meet Ruby Scribblez . . .

Ruby's a roving reporter for *Shrillboard Magazine*. If you want to know the hottest gossip in the Monstropolis, she's the gal to ask. Take it from us, Ruby knows everything! Although she's super-connected to the M-list now, she started her career as a label writer for Yukea!

Meet The Moshi MonStars

The Moshi MonStars are Monstro City's hottest band - period! Fans can't get enough of their music, queuing up to visit the YowYow theatre just to gaze at the pawprints they left in the monstercrete outside! Don't get too close however. Despite all the MonStar's success, you couldn't meet six clumsier monsters!

Meet Simon Growl . . .

You need skin thicker than Rocky the Baby Blockhead if you want to hang out with Simon Growl. He will tell you exactly what he thinks at all times. Funnily enough, he never seems to think nice things! He's been voted Monstro City's top talent judge three times in a row. No one's had the courage yet to tell him that he only wins the award because he's the only talent scout in town!

Meet Zack Binspin . . .

Moptop Tweenybop, Zack Binspin comes from Brashcan Alley but can usually be spotted hanging out at the Sandy Drain hotel, surrounded by fans desperate to get their hands on a lock of his lovely hair.

ZACK

Now that I'm back from the back of beyond, I really don't need all my explorer gear. Let's head over to Sludge Street. There's a shop there called Dodgy Dealz that will pay cold hard Rox for good equipment.

I've taken a look at all your wares and I think we can do a deal little Moshi momma. Let's make it interesting shall we? I'll offer you two deals – it's down to you which one you choose. one's a fair price, and one is – well, you'll see.

Dodgy Dealz

Pick A Deal

Work out Sly Chance's tricky sums and help Snuffy cut the best deal.

DEAL A
I, Sly Chance, will purchase Snuffy Hookum's assorted explorer's equipment for the grand total of . . .

$10 + 10 \div 10 \times 10 - 10 =$ _____ $\times 2 - 2 \div 2 + 2 \times 10 =$

____ Rox

DEAL B
I, Sly Chance, will purchase Snuffy Hookum's assorted explorer's equipment for the grand total of . . .

$1,000 - (800 \div 1 \times 1 - 100 + 40 \times 2 - 80) =$

_____ Rox

SNUFFY'S SHOPPING

· · · · · · · · · ·

A picture frame
Rainbow Shades
A Disco Ball
A Magic Wand
Build-a-Human Big Nose (well, why not?)

Thanks for your help. Let's hit the shops! I've written a list of things I'd like to buy today. Can you help me by looking in the store windows and totting up how much I need to spend? No time-wasting at the Games Starcade!

Horrods

60 Rox

· 24 Rox

35 Rox

118 Rox · 14 Rox · 100 Rox

MARKETPLACE
Monstro City

NOW OPEN!

88 Rox

101 Rox

38 Rox

FOR RENT

Hmmm up for rent, eh? Bit dilapidated, but I've stayed in worse. I'll bear it in mind.

TOTAL TO PAY =

.... Rox

27

SUPER DUPER SURPRISE!

Woah! What's that in the sky? Oh no! It's Dr. Strangeglove in Scare Force One, up to no good again! Let's dash into the volcano for cover, if we're lucky we may even run into Elder Furi. He's the smartest, wisest, oldest and crustiest monster in the whole Monster Universe. What he doesn't know, isn't worth knowing! Elder Furi is in charge of the Super Moshis – a crack Moshi peace-keeping force – I'm a huge fan!

Snuffy, I've been expecting you. Taking shelter from Strangeglove's airship are we? Very sensible. Since I know everything, I expect you've been telling your friend about the Super Moshis. Excellent! I took the liberty of preparing a little quiz to test your SM memory. All you have to do is match the mission description to the correct name!

SUPER MOSHI MISSIONS

MISSIONS

1. Missing Moshling Egg
2. Voyage under Potion Ocean
3. Strangeglove From Above
4. Candy Catastrophe
5. Pop Goes The Boo Hoo
6. Super Moshiversity Challenge
7. 20,000 Leagues Under The Fur
8. Spooktacular Spectacular
9. Snow Way Out
10. Super Weapon Showdown

FILE NOTES

A When the Super Moshi team arrive at Simon Growl's exclusive party, their super hero senses are tingling before they even walk through the front door!

B A fully monsterised airship and an evil genius are not a good mix! The Super Moshis flew into action after a call to stop Strangeglove from terrorising Fluffies in the clouds!

C With Elder Furi missing, purple smoke pumping out of the volcano and scant few clues, it's a desperate situation! The team needed to be at their super-est to solve this tricky mission!

D The Super Moshis called on one of their friends to solve this mystery – good 'ol Cap'n Buck! The villain stole fish and other watery creepies from the beach before running back to his HQ. But why?

E An evil form of disgustingly sickly sweet candy has been giving Moshis the tummy grubbles. Super Moshis are soon on the case to stop the baddie responsible for Dastardly Delights Candy.

F Buster Bumblechops is reporting that a strange egg has been stolen from his home, probably by Strangeglove! The crooked crook has left some clues for the SM team to go on. They solved the crime, could you?

G A epic mission begins when new baddies Sprockett and Hubbs hit the city! Do Elder Furi's crew have the power to take them on, reverse Strangeglove's Glumpatron and defeat C.L.O.N.C.'s Super Weapon?

H A scholarship to a super-exclusive Moshiversity has to be a good thing, right? Wrong! Nothing about the place is as it seems. This is one of the creepiest Super Moshi missions!

I There's trouble afoot when a famous Glitzy Boo Hoo loses her voice! Buster Bumblechops suspects foul play. Time for the SM crew to investigate!

J There are whispers that C.L.O.N.C. has set up a base on Mount Sillimanjaro, but what could the organisation be up to? Could the rumours that the villains are busy building a Monstro Super Weapon be true?

I'M GONNA GET YOU!

KRAKKABLOW.OUT!

There was no denying it – I was in a tight spot. Most Moshling Hunters would have surrendered in the squint of an eye, but not me! Snuffy Hookums wasn't going down without a fight . . .

I weighed up my options. I had been dragged to what looked like an abandoned fairground, tied to a stake and dunked in a cauldron. Quick as a flash I used the stake to pogo stick outta that cooking pot. I needed to catch up with IGGY, fast!

WANNA TRACK SNUFFY AND IGGY'S PROGRESS THROUGH THE FOOTHILLS OF MOUNT KRAKKABLOWA? GRAB A FRIEND AND GET READY TO PLAY!

START

1

2

3

4

Stop to explore the fairground. Go back to 3.

5

6

7

Dodge a Woolly Pink Hoodoo ambush. Move forward 5 spaces.

8

9

10

11

12

13

14

15

16

Fall into an underground cave. Go back to 13.

17

18

19

20

21

22

Flaming lava stream up ahead! Miss a turn.

23

24

25

26

27

ERUPTION! Go back to the start.

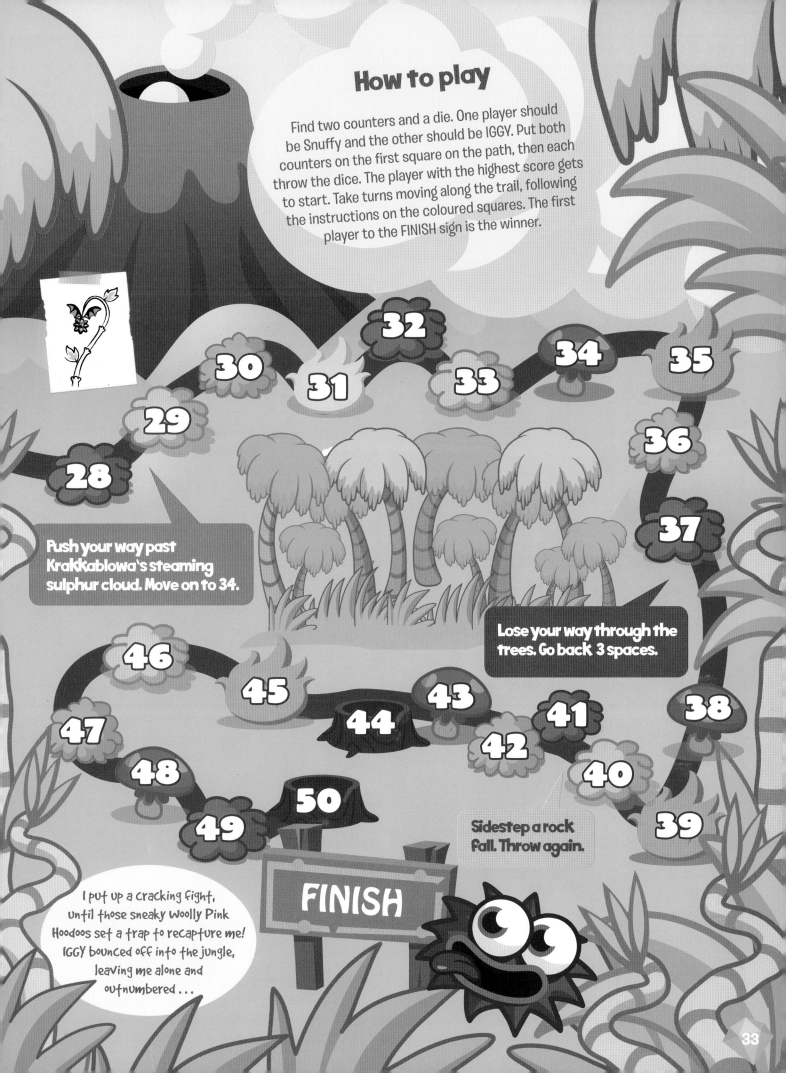

How to play

Find two counters and a die. One player should be Snuffy and the other should be IGGY. Put both counters on the first square on the path, then each throw the dice. The player with the highest score gets to start. Take turns moving along the trail, following the instructions on the coloured squares. The first player to the FINISH sign is the winner.

Push your way past Krakkablowa's steaming sulphur cloud. Move on to 34.

Lose your way through the trees. Go back 3 spaces.

Sidestep a rock fall. Throw again.

I put up a cracking fight, until those sneaky Woolly Pink Hoodoos set a trap to recapture me! IGGY bounced off into the jungle, leaving me alone and outnumbered . . .

FINISH

MUCH, MUCH LATER . . .

SIGH. NEXT!

WHAT THE -? IGGY?!

SSSHH.

ERK!

KNDYFLOZ! *STRANGER!*

STRANGERS!!

CHOMP

CHOMP!

YOU'RE GONNA HAVE TO LET ME CATCH YOU IGGY . . .

. . . I PROMISE TO LET YOU GO ONCE I'M BACK IN MONSTRO CITY!

River Deep, Mountain High

Since parting company with Buster, I've travelled far and wide from the top of the Yappalatian Mountains to the boiling oil swamps of Greasy Geezer. Some of the places I've been are as interesting as the Moshlings that brought me there! Take a look at my field notes on the best and worst.

Barmy Swami Jungle

Snuggly Tiger Cubs are fascinating. To camouflage themselves, they paint stripes on their fur in inka-inka juice! Luckily they have found an ingenious way around the difficulty in disguising themselves - they've made the Barmy Swami Jungle, the densest and most forbidding forest ever, their home! I could team a bright red top hat with neon socks and still be invisible there!

Jeepers

Barmy Swami Jungle

Meringue Meadow

Some of my best adventures hunting for Moshlings have happened when I've been tracking Fluffies. Apart from being impossibly sweet, the places they call home are without fail, adora-bubble. None more so than Dipsy the Dinky Dreamcloud, who hails from Meringue Meadow. Everything from the trees to the grass is softer than the back of a ShiShi's neck! I recall having the best nap of my life under a pillow tree there.

Dipsy

Meringue Meadow

Old Knackersville

This pic was taken when I was on the prowl for Priscilla the Princess Pony. I hunted around every swanky stream and hoity-toity hill I could think of without any luck. In the end, I read an old book Buster once gave me. In it, he described how despite their grand behaviour, Princess Ponies actually hail from a growl-and-you'll-miss-it meadowland called Old Knackersville, not far from Gluey Gulch! Who'd have thought it, eh?

Priscilla

Old Knackersville

Westmonster Abbey

Westmonster Abbey

Not all of my expeditions were into the deepest darkest jungles and hard-to-reach hideaways. Very occasionally, my hunt led me into cities and towns. One day I was on the trail of Mini Ben, the Teeny Ticktock. I had to roam every cobbled street of Growldon Town before I spotted one! It was tottering along the banks of the River Groans, just beside Westmonster Abbey.

Mini Ben

Sherlock Nook

This is one of the toughest places I've ever visited! I'd been on the lookout for an Undercover Yap Yap for sometime before I found one, quite by chance, playing with an Oochie Poochie in Uppity Meadow. Knowing that McNulty comes from Sherlock Nook in the Waggytail Hollow, I thought I'd take her back to her home. What a palaver that turned out to be! The Nook doesn't appear on any map and Yap Yap's are tight-lipped about the location. If I hadn't snuck up on her, I'm sure she would have run away!

McNulty

Sherlock Nook

How to draw
moshlings™

Tracking down thrilling new Moshlings is all very well - **PROVING** your sightings can pose an even bigger challenge! I once spent a marvellous evening sipping bonga-coladas with a COCOLOCO, but no one in Monstro City believed a word of it when I got home and told the tale! I had to hack all the way back to the Hoohah Husk Tree where we'd met and snatch this sketch of the Naughty Nutter before my discovery was confirmed.

Now I don't even hop out of my hammock without packing a sketchbook and colouring pencils. Pourquoi? Because, dear Moshling lover, you never know where you might come across a splendiferous new species!

Sketching Secrets

Next time you're roaming the Monstrosphere, take a minute to fill your field notes with sketches of the beasties that you come across. Remember - **a picture tells a thousand words!** If you don't draw what you see, your pals won't have a clueKoo who or what you tracked down.

Quick on the draw
Can't get started? Don't burst a blood vessel! Just take a minute to **churn out a few tiny doodles** of your new Moshling friend. These rough scribbles might not look right, but they'll help you **plan how to tackle your picture** and get off first base!

Pencils and peepers
When you've found your Moshling subject, **study it carefully.** Take care to draw in the **important details** that make it unique. Whether it's Big Bad Bill's eye patch or Liberty's heart tiara - **every distinguishing mark matters!**

Sum it up

Moshlings can be **wriggly little critters** at the best of times!
Try and pick a pose that sums them up best. How about showing
IGGY chomping on a cursor or Humphrey snoring in the sun?

Green, tangerine and everything in between

What would Scamp be without his rubbery green suit? Not a
Froggie Doggie, that's for sure! When it comes to bringing
your sketch to life, **a bit of colour makes all the difference.**
Choose your shades carefully – the colours will help you
identify your Moshling when you look it up later.

The critters in these
stunning sketches are
super rare, spotted in
lost and lonely habitats
many leagues away from
Monstro City. I just wish
I spied them myself . . .

Eye-Popping, Pencil-Dropping Pictures

My Moshling hunter pals have sent me a wodge of
ROARsome new drawings. Check them out!

Micro Dave
isaissa

Yoka
whymymollie2000

T.O.A.S.T.Y
zombiedude8831

King Toot
darciegirl123

39

TOO RARE TO SHARE

Can you keep a secret?
During my 1,882 days out in the wilds, I got to see
(and run away from) all sort of Moshlings – some of them very
rare indeed. In my journey from the fiery top of Mount Krakkablowa,
through Make Believe Valley, across Divinity Island, up fancy streets like
Ooh La Lane and everywhere in between, I've seen Moshlings of every
shape and size. I've been just itching to tell someone about them!

Let me show you the scrapbook I made about the ultra rarest, most
unique, and utterly fangtastic Moshlings ever. Just promise
you won't go blabbing!

Wurley the Twirly Tiddlycopter

CATEGORY: a Techie and an ultra-rare one at that.

NOTES: Very lucky to have seen this tin-skinned flier. Twirly Tiddlycopters are great at transporting Rox from place to place, so they're always in demand. After waiting for three days, (or was it six?!) hidden directly in front of Hangar Eight-and-a-half, the conditions were finally perfect for Tiddlycopter spotting.

I heard them long before I could see them as Twirly Tiddlycopters hum classical music while they fly. Had to be quick with my camera to snap them, as they're crazy about doing loop-the-loops. I don't know how they keep their dinner down!

Ingenious motory-rotory flying helmet takes wurley high above the clouds. Note to self - must get myself a hat like that!

Tin flying jacket, strong but no good in the rain as the rivets rust quicker than IGGY up a gloop pipe!

Plinky the Squeezy TinkleHuff

Be careful. Tickling in the wrong direction will have them hiccupping completely out of tune.

CATEGORY: one of the most elusive Tunies

NOTES: Couldn't believe my luck, spotting one of these little softies. I was strolling through Polka Park when, by chance, I stumbled across it. At first Plinky was very nervous, but I found that I could calm it down by giving the keys a little tickle. The next thing I knew, Plinky was huffing out the most beautiful tune this side of Mount Sillimanjaro!

Tinkling tunes isn't the only thing Squeezy Tinklehuffs do when you tickle them. They can bounce higher than an Oochie Poochie too!

Nipper the Titchy Trundlebot

CATEGORY: a Techie

NOTES: I was having real trouble putting my tent up on the bumpy floor of the Quivering Quarry when help came from an unlikely source. An Ultra-Rare Titchy Trundlebot trundled over, cleared a pile of boulders bigger than Buster Bumblechops' moustache to leave a perfect tent-sized space. My camp was set up, lickety split!

The flexiest, stretchiest arms I've ever seen on a Moshling! Made mincemeat of massive, mammoth boulders.

Caterpillar-clad tootsies mean there isn't a terrain in the Moshisphere Nipper can't tame!

Blingo the Flashy Fox

CATEGORY: definitely one of the Secrets

NOTES: How I managed to spot a Flashy Fox still amazes me. Walking through the Hipsta Hills I noticed the shiniest, sparkliest sight I'd ever peeped. The closer I got, the brighter it became. Suddenly, the pile of sparkles spoke, I nearly jumped out of my skin! "Wannaborrowmyshades?" it said, lightening fast. "WannaWobble-ade? Udigwotsgoingdown?!" I took the sunglasses I was offered (but not the Wobble-ade!) and popped them on. Suddenly I could see that I was talking to the funkiest, flashiest fox covered in blingo bling!

Flashy foxes never go anywhere without their boomboxes so they can rap along to their favourite tunes.

Never mind being too cool for school, a flashy fox would freeze one solid! In fact, the only way to make them lose their cool is to try and touch their shades. Be prepared to be told off if you dare to try!

Snuffy's BIG Belly Laughs

What do you do with a green Luvli?
Put it in the sun until it ripens!

I'm super-serious about studying Moshlings, but I also love a laugh! Over the years I've spent out in the wild, I've run into some of the giggliest, most chuckleful jokers in the whole Monstroverse! Here are my fave howlers. Bet you can't make it to the end without snorting!

A snooty Monstro City resident was visiting the Googenheim. **"Bah! I suppose this picture of a hideous monster is what you call modern art,"** he blabbed. **"No, sir,"** replied the assistant. **"That's what we call a mirror."**

How do Poppet parents begin their fairy tales?
"Once upon a slime!"

A monster owner went to the doctors and complained that he had swallowed a monster whole. Nothing the doctor could say would change his mind. So, the doctor put him to sleep and told him he was going to remove it. Instead of giving him an operation, the doctor simply invited Snozzle Wobbleson round and waited for the owner to wake up. **"Nothing more to worry about,"** the doctor said. **"We operated on you and took him out." "Who are you trying to kid?"** said the monster owner. **"The one I swallowed was blue!"**

Did you hear about the Zommer with twelve arms and no legs?
He's all fingers and thumbs.

I know a Moshi who has an extra pair of hands. He keeps them in a handbag!

What happens if a Furi sits in front of you at the cinema?
You miss most of the film!

Dr. Strangeglove: "Sweet Tooth, have you seen my new invention? It's a pill made half from glue and half from aspirin."
Sweet Tooth: "What's it for?"
Dr. Strangeglove: "I've got a splitting headache!"

How does Diavlo cure a sore throat?
Easy, just spend five minutes gargoyling!

PUZZLE PALACE

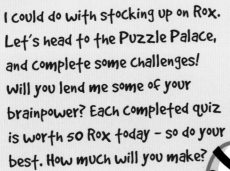

I could do with stocking up on Rox. Let's head to the Puzzle Palace, and complete some challenges! Will you lend me some of your brainpower? Each completed quiz is worth 50 Rox today – so do your best. How much will you make?

SNUFFY'S SUDOKU

Do you know your numbers? Find out with this Sudoku game. The object is to fill in the empty squares with any number from one to nine. One mega-important rule: Each number should appear only once in each row, column and three by three square.

				3	1	5		
		6		9			4	
3				4			8	
5		7			6	8	9	
	3		7		5		1	
	8	1	9			7		4
5			6					7
1					9			
	4	8	7		1			

SPOT THE DIFFERENCE

There are eight monster differences between these two pictures of Buck, Gail and Blurp. Can you find them all?

44

WHERE'S ZACK BINSPIN?

Quick! Monster pop star Zack has accidentally wandered out of the V.I.M. section of the Underground Disco. Now he's lost on the crowded dance floor with all the 'normal' monsters! Can you find him?

MATCH THAT 'TACHE!

Moustaches are über-popular in Monstro City. Have you been paying attention to all the furry lips out there? Draw lines to match each 'tache to the correct owner!

QUICK MOSHLING WORD SEARCH

Eight Moshling names are hidden in the grid below, can you find them all in under two minutes?

P	U	R	D	Y	N	V	G	Y	S
I	D	O	Q	O	P	O	I	A	N
H	W	C	A	L	I	O	N	K	O
A	Q	K	F	O	W	K	G	L	O
N	K	Y	L	C	C	Z	E	F	K
S	E	R	L	A	M	Z	R	R	U
E	X	L	U	R	Q	V	S	E	M
L	V	Q	X	G	W	D	N	P	S
R	J	K	V	K	K	B	A	S	T
D	G	A	A	R	P	E	P	P	Y

PURDY **ROCKY** **DJ QUACK**

SNOOKUMS **GINGERSNAP** **PEPPY**

HANSEL **CALI**

TOTAL ROX POT

Gift Island QUIZ

Ooh, that last word search has befuddled my brain! Let's recover with some retail therapy! I haven't been to Gift Island in ooh 1,882 days. My old pal Skeeter Rydell will be able to help us out!

Hi Snuffs, welcome to Gift Island! We have the perfect treat here for every kind of monster, so you'll definitely be able to find something nifty. Feel free to wander wherever you want. I've got another delivery to do so I can't show you round myself. It's probably for the best though - I always end up getting lost anyway! You can learn about the island by completing this quiz as you go.

1 What direction does the train on Gift Island travel around the mountain?

A. Clockwise   B. Anti-clockwise

2 Presents are delivered to The Port by boat, true or false?

A. True   B. False

3 What creature lives in the sea between The Port and Gift Island?

A. A shark   B. A whale

4 Which Roarker has the job of counting presents?

A. Casper   B. Jasper

5 Shy Bert has been working on the Island for ages, but likes to keep himself to himself. What is his pet hate?

A. Early mornings   B. Being disturbed

6 Bert's always sweating, do you know why?

A. He's out of shape 'cos he only eats Roarberry Cheesecake   B. He's scared that he'll fall in the water and be eaten by a monster-munching jellyfuzz

7 Elwood works on the island, too. You'll be able to spot him by the bandage on his head. Why does he wear it?

A. He keeps hitting his shovel into his face   B. He thinks it makes him look like a ninja

8 Clutch is the longest-serving member of the Gift Island staff. How long has he worked here for?

A. Over twenty years   B. Over thirty years

9 Why has Clutch lingered so long?

A. He loves smiling monster owners   B. He's forgotten that he's allowed to go home

10 A RoboDonut Roarker helps manage the huge amount of pressies on the island. What is his name?

A. Clem   B. Roy G. Biv

MONSTER STYLE FILE

So much has changed while I have been away! I feel like I need some tips on getting the right look. Luckily I know just the person to help me out – Preen Magazine cover girl, Mizz Snoots! Mizz is the face of Horrods. What she doesn't know about style you could write on the back of a Moshling seed!

Hi Snuffy.
Great to see you, I've been hearing loads about your trip. I've seen every fashion you can imagine and I'd love to lend a hand. Here are my five top style tips . . .

MIZZ SNOOTS' STYLE FILE

Step one
CONFIDENCE

If you believe in yourself, and have confidence in how you look, you can pull off any style you choose.

Step two
COLOUR

Monstro City is a pretty colourful place! Make colour your friend and you're sure to stand out.

Step three
PASSION

Get excited by style and care about what you wear! Monsters are always impressed by someone who puts effort into how they look. Go for it!

Step four
TRENDS

No one remembers someone who follows trends and fashions. But if you're the one who's starting a new look, you'll definitely stick in their Moshi minds.

Step five
BE YOURSELF

What's cooler than clothes, bling, colour or even fashion, is being yourself. Wearing trendy clothes is great, but there's nothing cooler than someone who isn't afraid to be who they are!

MOSHLING SPOTTING

The best lesson Buster Bumblechops ever taught me is that successful Moshling spotters manage to get the little critters to come to them. Here are my tricks for attracting the rarest of the rare!

GURGLE

Performing Flappasaurus Moshlings are born show-offs, so I find a spot in Crazy Canyons and start applauding as loudly as I can. They can't resist performing for an enthusiastic audience, even if it is only an audience of one!

Seed secrets:

 DRAGON FRUIT **RED**
 LOVE BERRIES **PURPLE**
 MAGIC BEANS **YELLOW**

BIG BAD BILL

Woolly Blue Hoodoos like to wander all over the jungle. Luckily, they don't like going off the beaten track or travelling at night, so find a hiding place on the main path and one should soon amble along!

Seed secrets:

 STAR BLOSSOM **BLUE**
 LOVE BERRIES **YELLOW**
 STAR BLOSSOM **BLACK**

SHISHI

Sneezing Pandas are one of the only Moshlings that are tempted most by something other than seeds. They're at their happiest aah-chooing in front of a monstrovision box. So simply set one up and wait!

Seed secrets:

 DRAGON FRUIT **RED**
 HOT SILLY PEPPERS **YELLOW**
 CRAZY DAISY **BLACK**

GENERAL FUZUKI

Warrior Wombats may look tough, but these little sleepyheads have a soft spot for comfy corners. Simply arrange a few scatter cushions, stay quiet and wait for them to arrive.

Seed secrets:

 HOT SILLY PEPPERS **RED**
 LOVE BERRIES **YELLOW**
 STAR BLOSSOM **PURPLE**

MAKE YOUR OWN GLOOP!

YOU WILL NEED

A mixing bowl
Cornflour
A tablespoon
A jug of water
Food colouring, green of course!
A mixing spoon

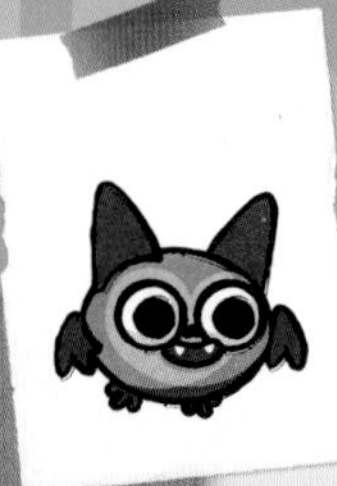

WHAT TO DO

1.

Make sure your bowl is clean and placed on a flat surface. Add some heaped spoonfuls of cornflour to your bowl. For your first batch, I'd recommend starting small, so about two tablespoons should do it. As you become an experienced Gloop producer you can use more.

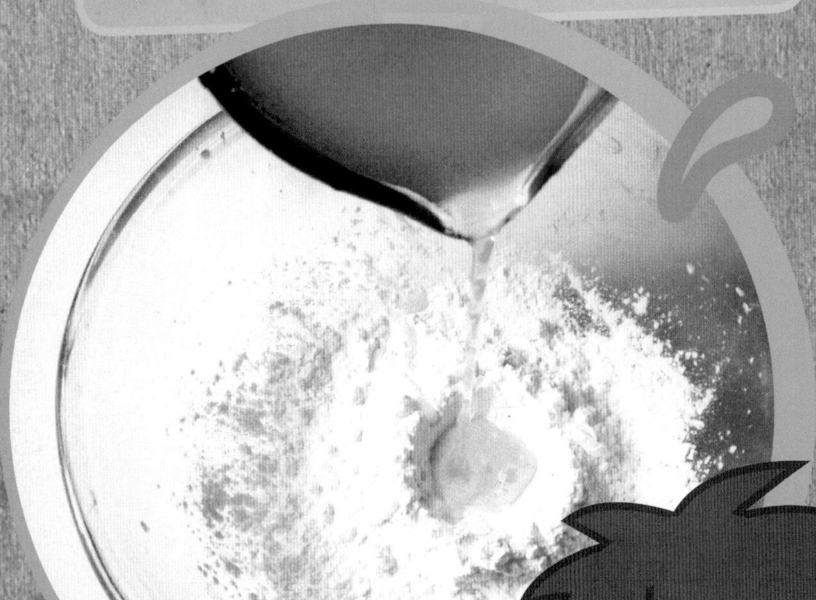

2.

2. Fill your jug with some cold water from the tap. Once you've filled your jug, add a few drops of your food colouring. Just a little is perfect, it's powerful stuff!

3.

Make a small well in the middle of your cornflour and pour a little of the coloured water in it. Now grab your spoon and start to slowly mix the water and cornflour together, moving in small circles. Don't mix too fast or it won't work.

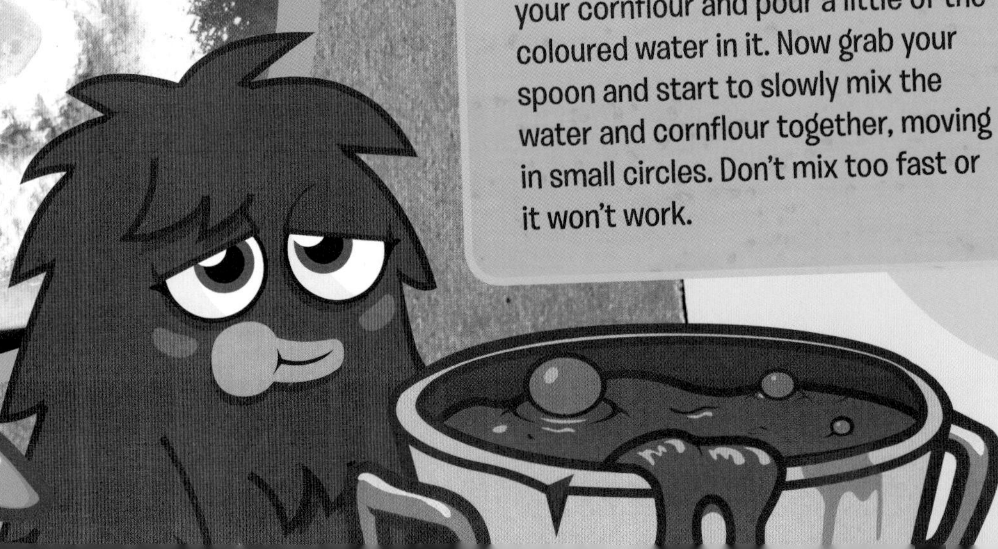

If there's one thing I've learned on my travels, it's that all Moshis and Moshlings need a little Gloop in their lives! We lurvvvve the stuff. The good news is that making your own batch is oh-so simple. Just follow these easy instructions and you'll soon have your own stockpile of gorgeous green Gloop!

4.

Once the water and cornflour are really well combined, add a little more water to the bowl and mix slowly again. Keep doing this until your mixture feels just like Gloop. Don't worry if it gets too watery, just sprinkle in a little more cornflour until you get the consistency you're after. If you've never handled Gloop before, it feels just like custard!

5.

Now things start to get interesting, it's time to check your Gloop for gooeyness! Gently tap the surface of your Gloop with a spoon! If it's made properly, your spoon should bounce off the surface as if you were hitting rubber. Now here's the clever bit. Stir it again and it should still feel like a liquid. Neat huh?!

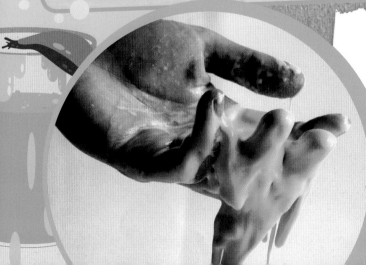

Congratulations! You're now a fully-fledged Super Glooper! Try rolling the magical substance into a ball in your hand and see how long it takes before it starts dripping between your fingers. Why not experiment with some different colours, changing the amounts of cornflour and water to devise your own brand of special, ultra rare goo? It's too gloopy to resist!

CANDY CANE CAVE CHASE

I've missed the Candy Cane Caves, they're just so sweet! I take care to never be too relaxed here however, because someone else likes these sugary bolt holes just as much as I do. Yep, you guessed it! The Caves are the haunt of choice of Sweet Tooth, Dr. Strangeglove's right-hand menace, and leading member of C.L.O.N.C.!

Can you help me find a safe route to the icky sticky candy cane caves? There's only one route that will lead me safely to the Cupcake Cavern and away from Sweet Tooth's sticky grasp. Can you find it?

MOSHI CUPCAKES

Phew, that was a close one, thanks! Now we've given Sweet-chops the slip, let's celebrate by going cupcake crazy! Bake a perfect cupcake, then decorate it and match it to your favourite Moshling. My mouth's watering already!

Yum, yum!
Time to colour
the cake in!

53

Photo fangtastic!

All that cake talk has made my tummy rumble! Sniff, sniff . . . what is that delish smell? If I didn't know better I'd say it was a dead ringer for Buster's secret recipe for campfire kebabs! Those cookouts of his used to be something special. Mmmm . . . This nosefest is so scrumptious, I think I'll sit here for a while and take a moment to stick some pics into my journal.

I'm very fussy about cataloguing my photos – Moshling hunting isn't just fun, fun, fun, you know! (Not 24/7 anyway, even I have to take time out to write my notes and wash my socks). Can you help write an interesting caption to each shot? It's been quite a busy day.

Day 1,882 – Back to Monstro City

Secret Solved!

Something tells me that I'm within a Waldo's whisker of uncovering the secret location of Buster's ranch! Could there really be a home-style cookout happening just around the corner? If my old partner's in the area, wild Moshlings won't keep me away!

USE THIS SPACE TO CRACK BUSTER'S PICTURE CODE.

-- -- ----- ----

---- ----- ------

---- ----- ------

---- -----

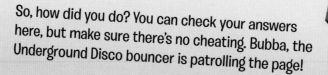

Answers

So, how did you do? You can check your answers here, but make sure there's no cheating. Bubba, the Underground Disco bouncer is patrolling the page!

Endpapers
FAMOUS FACES

Mrskerney - Harry Potter
Queenmoshi1220 - Cat Woman
Chocol8cracker - Lady Gaga
Moshi1024555 - Katy Perry
Billandcag - Marily Monroe
Diamondintellect - Jackie Chan
Mouse127921 - Princess Kate

Page 9
MONSTERS IN SIGHT!
1. Zommer   3. Katsuma   5. Poppet
2. Furi   4. Diavlo   6. Luvli

Pages 12-13
CAP'N BUCK'S PORT TOUR
Buck's code: **MY NAME IS CAP'N BUCK**

Page 16
FRENZY IN FLUTTERBY FIELD
There are 92 Flutterbies.

The rare Flutterby is

Page 19
ROAR ALL ABOUT IT!
Intrepid Moshling hunter Snuffy Hookums dramatically returned to Monstro City today after **1,882** days on her own in the wild! Her reappearance has put paid to rumours that she had been eaten by a tribe of dangerous Moshlings somewhere near Mount **Krakkablowa**.

Hookums' incredible return will be celebrated with a monstermental boogie party at the **Underground Disco**. Crowds have been warned to get there early to avoid being left out in the cold.

Page 20
PETE AND LILA'S POTTY PICNIC
Glump Hunt

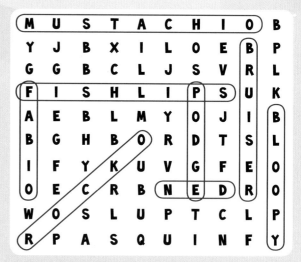

The other Glumps are:
1. PIRATE PONG   3. SQUIFF
2. FREAKFACE   4. BLACK JACK

Pages 26-27
DODGY DEALZ
Pick A Deal
DEAL A
10 + 10 ÷ 10 x 10 - 10 = **10** x 2 -2 ÷2 + 2 x 10 = **110 Rox**

DEAL B
1,000 - (800 ÷ 1 x 1 - 100 + 40 x 2 - 80) = **400 Rox**

SNUFFY'S SHOPPING
TOTAL TO PAY = **293 Rox**

Pages 28-29
SUPER DUPER SURPRISE!
Super Moshi Missions
1.F, 2.D, 3.B, 4.E, 5.I, 6.H, 7.C, 8.A, 9.J, 10.G

Pages 44-45
PUZZLE PALACE
Snuffy's Sudoku

2	4	8	6	3	1	5	7	9
1	7	6	5	9	8	3	4	2
3	9	5	2	4	7	6	8	1
5	2	7	4	1	6	8	9	3
4	3	9	7	8	5	2	1	6
6	8	1	9	2	3	7	5	4
8	5	3	1	6	9	4	2	7
7	1	2	3	5	4	9	6	8
9	6	4	8	7	2	1	8	7

Spot The Difference

Where's Zac Binspin?

Match That 'Tache!

Quick Moshling Word Search

P	U	R	D	Y	N	V	G	Y	S
I	D	O	Q	O	P	O	I	A	N
H	W	C	A	L	I	O	N	K	O
A	Q	K	F	O	W	K	G	L	O
N	K	Y	L	C	C	Z	E	F	K
S	E	R	L	A	M	Z	R	R	U
E	X	L	U	R	Q	V	S	E	M
L	V	Q	X	G	W	D	N	P	S
R	J	K	V	K	K	B	A	S	T
D	G	A	A	R	P	E	P	P	Y

Pages 46-47
GIFT ISLAND QUIZ
1. A, 2. B, 3. B, 4. A, 5. B, 6. B, 7. A, 8. B, 9. A, 10. A.

Pages 52-53
CANDY CANE CAVE CHASE
Monster-Mazing Cave Maze

Page 55
SECRET SOLVED!
GO THREE TIMES ROUND MONSTRO CITY THEN FOLLOW YOUR NOSE

Pages 56-57
RANCH REUNION